ZOË KRAVITZ

X-MEN'S AMAZING ANGEL

SANDY DONOVAN

Lerner Publications Company
MINNEAPOLIS

Lerner Publications Company
A division of Lerner Publishing Group, Inc.
241 First Avenue North
Minneapolis, MN 55401 U.S.A.

Website address: www.lernerbooks.com

Library of Congress Cataloging-in-Publication Data

Donovan, Sandra, 1967–
    Zoë Kravitz : X-Men's amazing angel / by Sandy Donovan.
       p.   cm. — (Pop culture bios: action movie stars)
    Includes index.
    ISBN 978-1-4677-0747-3 (lib. bdg. : alk. paper)
    1. Kravitz, Zoë, 1988– —Juvenile literature. 2. Actors—United
States—Biography—Juvenile literature. 3. Singers—United States—
Biography—Juvenile literature. I. Title.
PN2287.K73D66 2013
791.4302'8092—dc23   2012022459

Manufactured in the United States of America
1 – PC – 12/31/12

INTRODUCTION
PAGE 4

CHAPTER ONE
GROWING UP FAMOUS
PAGE 6

CHAPTER TWO
LAUNCHING A CAREER
PAGE 12

CHAPTER THREE
BRIGHT FUTURE
PAGE 22

ZOË PICS!   28
SOURCE NOTES   30
MORE ZOË INFO   30
INDEX   31

FROM LEFT: Michael Fassbender, Zoë Kravitz, and James McAvoy attend a film event.

INTRODUCTION

Zoë and other X-Men cast members pose at the film's premiere on May 25, 2011.

It's May 25, 2011. Zoë Kravitz shimmers in her Alexander Wang dress. On her arm is her *X-Men: First Class* costar and date for the evening, Michael Fassbender. The two are outside New York's famed Ziegfeld Theatre. They are just about to attend the premiere of their *X-Men* movie.

This is Zoë's big night. As the daughter of famous parents, she's been around paparazzi all her life. Her own acting career has also brought her plenty of attention. *X-Men: First Class* is her tenth film. Still, most of her other roles were in artsy, independent films. *X-Men* is her first major Hollywood movie. It's catching all kinds of media attention.

As the paparazzi's cameras flash, Zoë gives her trademark half-smile. She and Michael wave at the gathered crowd. Zoë can't believe how many people have come out to see her! But she'd better get used to the attention. After all, this talented and beautiful star's career is headed in only one direction: up!

Zoë shows off a new short haircut in July 2012.

Zoë's dad holds her hand tight!

Baby Zoë and her parents in 1989

CHAPTER ONE

GROWING UP FAMOUS

Zoë gets a big hug from her papa.

Zoë Isabella Kravitz was born on December 1, 1988. She was born into pop culture royalty. Her mom, Lisa Bonet, was one of the world's most famous TV stars. Most people knew her as the teen daughter Denise Huxtable on the TV series *The Cosby Show*. At the time, *The Cosby Show* was the United States' number one rated show. And Lisa was a big fan favorite. She even starred in her own spin-off series, *A Different World.*

Lisa married up-and-coming rocker Lenny Kravitz on her twentieth birthday in November 1987. They had Zoë just about one year later. The family split their time between New York and Los Angeles. Soon after Zoë was born, Lenny's career took off. He released his first album, *Let Love Rule,* in 1989.

FAMILY ROOTS

Coincidentally, both Zoë's mom and dad grew up with one Jewish parent and one African American parent. Lisa has said that their similar backgrounds were part of what attracted her to Lenny.

Life with Mom

When Zoë was five, her parents divorced. Zoë lived with her mother for several years. Lisa cut back on acting so she could have more time to spend with her daughter. She felt this was the best decision for her and Zoë. Zoë later said how much she admired her mom's decision. "She walked away from being famous, because she didn't really care about it," Zoë remarked in 2011. "She is the most true artist I have met. She doesn't change for anybody. And the fact that she's my mom is just so cool!"

Zoë Kravitz and Lisa Bonet in 2011

Zoë's mom, Lisa Bonet (FAR LEFT), played Denise Huxtable on the popular TV series The Cosby Show. Here she poses with the show's cast.

Life with Dad

At the age of eleven, Zoë began spending more time at her dad's house. By the time she was a teen, her dad was a chart-topping star. He was known for his funky, soulful, 1960s-style music. And he was also known for his crazy outfits. Zoë remembers that her dad was fun but strict. "My dad was brought up very old school, very strict—'Yes, ma'am, yes, sir,' " she explained. "So he's wearing leather pants and a boa, but he would be like, 'Did you do your chores today?', or, 'That dress is too short.' " Having Lenny Kravitz for a dad sometimes made life very interesting!

Zoë's dad, Lenny Kravitz, performs in 1992 in one of his trademark crazy outfits.

Making It

Zoë attended Rudolph Steiner High School on New York City's Upper East Side. She loved her time there. Chatty and outgoing, Zoë had tons of friends. She liked to goof around with them and also just hang out.

Zoë's expressive personality, plus the influence of her artsy parents, drew her to explore acting in high school. By then, Zoë knew she'd love to see her name in the credits for a film someday. But Zoë didn't just want fame. She wanted to be a serious artist. With that in mind, she decided to see if she could land any auditions for films with smart, creative scripts. Zoë knew that getting film auditions of any kind would probably be a long shot. But her parents' connections helped her out.

Zoë in high school back in 2004

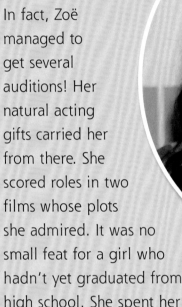

In fact, Zoë managed to get several auditions! Her natural acting gifts carried her from there. She scored roles in two films whose plots she admired. It was no small feat for a girl who hadn't yet graduated from high school. She spent her senior year filming while also finishing up her degree.

Zoë attends a movie premiere in 2007, the year she graduated from high school.

Zoë (RIGHT) rehearses a movie scene with fellow actor Chanel Farrell.

CHAPTER TWO

LAUNCHING A CAREER

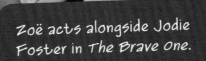

Zoë acts alongside Jodie Foster in *The Brave One*.

The films that Zoë made in high school came out in 2007. Audiences enjoyed both *No Reservations*, a romantic comedy in which Zoë plays the babysitter of a young orphan, and *The Brave One*, in which Zoë plays a girl who has to fend for herself on the streets.

Even with her big-time success in two films, Zoë was committed to becoming a better actor. She decided to study acting in college. She enrolled in acting school at the State University of New York.

Independent Artist

Zoë's love for intelligent scripts only grew as she studied acting. She chose to mostly pursue roles in independent films. In 2008, Zoë appeared in *Birds of America*, an indie starring Matthew Perry. The film appeared at the Sundance Film Festival.

Zoë played the role of Charlotte in *No Reservations*, featuring Aaron Eckhart and Catherine Zeta-Jones.

SUNDANCE

Sundance is one of the largest film events of the year. At this festival in Salt Lake City, Utah, the biggest Hollywood stars mingle with a crop of movie newcomers. Why do they all come to Sundance? Partly to see and be seen. They also come to catch a glimpse of up-and-coming movies. Throughout the festival, the latest U.S. and International independent films are shown in invitation-only theaters.

The following year, Zoë costarred in another independent film, *The Greatest,* with Pierce Brosnan and Susan Sarandon. *The Greatest* premiered at Sundance in 2009. Zoë also filmed *Yelling to the Sky* that year. In that movie, she played Sweetness O'Hara, a troubled seventeen-year-old girl from Queens, New York.

Zoë and the *Yelling to the Sky* director (RIGHT) pose with a graffiti artist (LEFT) in front of artwork he created to honor the film.

Musical Side

Acting wasn't Zoë's only interest. She has also always loved music and music videos. Around the time she worked on *Yelling to the Sky*, she scored a starring role in the video for Jay-Z's single *I Know*. She was also asked to sing in will.i.am's video *We Are the Ones*. Will.i.am made this video in support of U.S. presidential candidate Barack Obama. Meanwhile, in early 2009, Zoë and three musicians she knew decided to start their own band called Elevator Fight. Within a year, the band proved itself by landing a gig at the famous South by Southwest music festival in Austin, Texas. Zoë sings lead vocals and cowrites most of Elevator Fight's music.

BFFs

Zoë considers rapper Jay-Z (RIGHT) one of her BFFs. The two artists love hanging out together. Other besties include designer Alexander Wang and actor Jennifer Lawrence. Zoë also goes way back with actor Olivia Thirlby. Olivia is best known for her role as Leah, best friend of the title character in the 2007 film *Juno*.

Zoë rocks out onstage with her band Elevator Fight.

Like her dad, Zoë listens to lots of different kinds of music. All of them influenced her as she worked to shape Elevator Fight. In 2009, Zoë told an interviewer about just a few of her many influences. "I listen to a lot of old music," she explained.

"Nina Simone, Jimi Hendrix, The Beatles. [And from] nowadays, Radiohead, Ray LaMontagne, [and] Feist." All of these artists' work guided Zoë as she helped to decide what kind of music Elevator Fight would make.

Fashion Forward

As the daughter of two fashion trendsetters, Zoë also has a major passion for fashion. She likes to pull together unique outfits to help her make a statement when she sings or gives an interview. Her fav spots to shop? Vintage stores and thrift shops. She's also been known to raid her parents' closets!

Zoë's sense of style has captured the media's attention. Her image is often splashed across the pages of trendy magazines. Zoë has even been invited to model for different mags. She's been in *Elle* and other fashion publications. She also starred in ads for designer and friend Alexander Wang.

Sporting fashionable duds, Zoë attends the 2012 Mercedes-Benz Fashion Week in New York City.

In addition, Zoë was the face for Vera Wang's perfume called Princess in 2009. A short time later, she represented a newer scent from Vera Wang called Preppy Princess.

Films and Festivals

By 2010, Zoë was famous for much more than just having famous parents. But she didn't slow down. That year, she appeared in three films. In *It's Kind of a Funny Story*, she plays a friend and occasional love interest to a suicidal teen. In *Twelve*, she plays a wealthy party girl from New York City's Upper East Side. And in *Beware the Gonzo*, she stars as a quirky high school newspaper columnist.

Zoë modeled for the Vera Wang Princess perfume.

Zöe with fellow cast member Ezra Miller in *Beware the Gonzo*

Making so many movies in one year meant that Zöe had a ton of events to attend. *Twelve* premiered at Sundance in 2010. That same year, *Beware the Gonzo* was shown at the Tribeca Film Festival.

Zöe on the set of *Twelve*

Zoë also began her work on *X-Men* in 2010. She played Angel Salvadore, a mutant with wings. *X-Men* was filmed in Europe, so Zoë moved to London for the filming. Although she missed her friends in New York and L.A., Zoë had an awesome time in Europe. Going to flea markets, eating out, and making new friends were her fav London activities.

Zoë in X-Men: First Class

It's not a boy—it's tattoos! "I'm kind of addicted," Zoë spills. "I have, like, eighteen or nineteen, but they're really small. I can't get a big one because of the film stuff." Zoë's first tattoo was a heart. But she gave her tatt a special twist. "You know in my name how I have the umlaut [the two dots] over the e?" she says. "Well, I have it over the heart, and that's to remind me to love myself."

Zoë stayed put in London into 2011. In late winter of that year, she took a side trip to Germany. *Yelling to the Sky* premiered at the Berlin International Film Festival then. Between the thrill of travel and the honor of seeing her work win praise, Zoë was living her dream life.

Zoë with her dad, Lenny Kravitz, at the Oscars

CHAPTER THREE

BRIGHT FUTURE

When *X-Men: First Class* blew up the box office in the summer of 2011, Zoë went from up-and-coming indie actor to certified Hollywood star. The movie earned more than $350 million worldwide. It sold out shows across the United States, Europe, and Asia.

And audiences absolutely *loved* Zoë! She was nominated for a Scream Award and a Teen Choice Award. Both were for the breakout female performance of 2011. On top of that, *Rolling Stone* magazine named her one of the Hottest Breakout Stars of 2011.

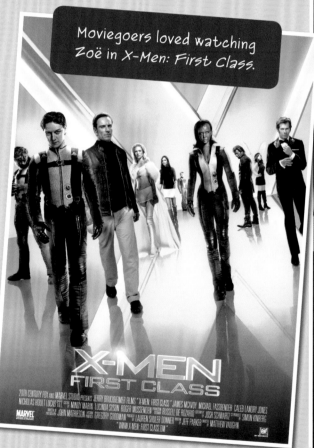

Moviegoers loved watching Zoë in *X-Men: First Class*.

Staying Grounded

Zoë's sudden fame in the mainstream film world changed her life dramatically. Suddenly everyone seemed to be following her every move. She was bombarded with requests for interviews and photo shoots. It was hard to make time for herself with everything she had going on. Still, Zoë made sure to carve out time to see family and friends. She kept especially close with her parents, who understand the pressures of fame. "We talk every day," Zoë said of her relationship with her parents. "I can literally tell them everything, which is great." Zoë's family has helped her stay grounded in the face of her enormous success.

Growing Family

Zoë's parents aren't the only family members that help her keep her sanity. Growing up, Zoë was an only child. But her mom had been involved with actor Jason Momoa since 2005, and

Lenny and Lisa help keep their daughter on the right track.

Zoë has said that she identifies with unusual and "out-there" characters in movies, like the winged, go-go-boot-wearing one she plays in *X-Men*. "I'm a total weirdo and have often felt like an outcast and a freak," Zoë spills. "[For me], playing a very accepted, normal person would actually be more interesting and difficult to do!"

the couple had a baby girl when Zoe was eighteen and a baby boy when Zoë was nineteen. Now Zoë loves being big sis to Lola Iolani Momoa and Nakoa-Wolf Manakauapo Namakaeha Momoa. She has tons of fun playing with her younger sibs!

Zoë has a blast with her mom and Lisa's partner, Jason Momoa (CENTER).

A Name for Herself

As the daughter of two pop-star parents, Zoë could have taken an easy route to success. She could have relied entirely on her parents' connections. But she prefers to challenge herself and prove that she has her own talents. As Zoë told *W* magazine, she likes taking movie parts that people might not expect to see her in. "My part in *The Brave One* was actually written for a blonde with a

ZOË'S BFs

Zoë's busy life doesn't always leave time for serious relationships. But she has connected with a few special guys. So whom has Zoë dated? Here's a peek.

Ben Foster: Zoë dated this *X-Men: The Last Stand* actor in 2008.

Michael Fassbender: Zoë dated her *X-Men: First Class* costar in early 2011.

Penn Badgley: By late summer 2011, Zoë was dating *Gossip Girl* star Penn Badgley. They've been spotted around town throughout 2012.

Zoë chats with Penn Badgley in October 2011.

European accent," she spilled. "My part in *It's Kind of a Funny Story* was originally written for an Asian girl. They

The supertalented Will Smith (LEFT) and Jaden Smith (RIGHT) will join Zoë in the movie *1000 A.E.*

didn't initially think of me for those roles. It's my job to change minds." Zoë certainly seems to have the skills to show directors she belongs in starring roles!

Zoë has no plans to slow down or stop challenging herself anytime soon. She's set to play Will Smith's daughter—and Jaden Smith's sister—in the 2013 sci-fi adventure *1000 A.E.* She also plans to keep writing songs, singing, modeling, and generally following her dreams. As far as whether fame will follow, Zoë says she tries not to worry about it. As she stated in one interview, "I'm in a very lucky position, because I've been around [fame] so long, I don't feel like I have to chase it." Zoë says she loves where she is in her career right now. "I feel good about the choices I've made, and I don't feel like I've let go of any of my values," she says. That passion and self-assurance seem likely to carry Zoë far.

Zoë with Rocsi (CENTER) and Terrence J (RIGHT), hosts of a popular video countdown show on the cable network BET

ZOË
PICS!

Zoë with Jimmy Fallon (RIGHT) on Late Night with Jimmy Fallon

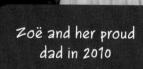

Zoë and her proud
dad in 2010

SOURCE NOTES

8 *Hello Beautiful*, "Zoë Kravitz in ASOS: On Best Friend Jay-Z & Uncomfortable 'It Girl' Title," June 1, 2011, http://hellobeautiful.com/1852505/zoe-kravitz-asos-magazine-july-2011 (June 12, 2012).

9 Ibid.

16 Just Jared, "Zoë Kravitz Interview—JustJared.com Exclusive," *Justjared.com*, January 26, 2009, http://www.justjared.com/2009/01/26/Zoë-kravitz-interview (May 1, 2012).

21 *ASOS*, "Pretty, Cool, Connected," July 2011, http://epub02.publitas.com/ASOS/10/magazine.php?spread=70 (July 16, 2012).

24 Ibid.

25 Christina Radish, "Ezra Miller and Zoë Kravitz Exclusive Interview: Beware the Gonzo," *Collider.com*, August 26, 2011, http://collider.com/ezra-miller-zoe-kravitz-beware-the-gonzo-interview/111259/#more-111259 (July 17, 2012).

26–27 *ASOS*, "Pretty, Cool, Connected."

27 Ibid.

MORE ZOË INFO

Facebook: Zoë Kravitz
http://www.facebook.com/pages/Zoe-kravitz/43886607775
Visit Zoë's FB home for all the latest on this talented performer.

IMDb: Zoë Kravitz
http://www.imdb.com/name/nm2368789
Check out Internet Movie Database to get fun deets on Zoë's life and work.

Krensky, Stephen. *Comic Book Century: The History of American Comic Books*. Minneapolis: Twenty-First Century Books, 2008. True *X-Men* fans won't want to miss this serious and in-depth look at the history of U.S. comics.

Krohn, Katherine. *Jennifer Lawrence: Star of The Hunger Games*. Minneapolis: Lerner Publications Company, 2012. Read the life story of Jennifer Lawrence, another key player in *X-Men*.

Marvel Comics
http://marvel.com
If you're into *X-Men*, you'll love this look at Marvel comics characters, books, and movies.

INDEX

Badgley, Penn, 26
Beware the Gonzo, 18–19
Birds of America, 13
Bonet, Lisa, 7, 24–25
Brave One, The, 13, 26–27

Elevator Fight, 15–16

Fassbender, Michael, 5, 26
Foster, Ben, 26

Greatest, The, 14

It's Kind of a Funny Story, 18, 27

Jay-Z, 15

Kravitz, Lenny, 7, 9, 16, 24

Lawrence, Jennifer, 15

Momoa, Jason, 24
Momoa, Lola Iolani, 25
Momoa, Nakoa-Wolf Manakauapo Namakaeha, 25

No Reservations, 13

1000 A.E., 27

Salvadore, Angel, 20
Sundance Film Festival, 14, 19

Thirlby, Olivia, 15
Twelve, 18–19

Wang, Alexander, 5, 15, 17

X-Men: First Class, 5, 20, 23, 26

Yelling to the Sky, 14–15, 21

PHOTO ACKNOWLEDGMENTS

The images in this book are used with the permission of: © Jamie McCarthy/WireImage/Getty Images, pp. 2, 5; © Jeff Kravitz/FilmMagic, Inc/Getty Images, pp. 3 (top), 6 (top left); © Stephen Lovekin/Getty Images, pp. 3 (bottom), 4 (bottom), 22 (bottom); © Dave M. Benett/Getty Images, p. 4 (top left); © Gary Gershoff/WireImage/Getty Images, p. 4 (top right); © Vinnie Zuffante/Getty Images, p. 6 (top right); © Neal Preston/CORBIS, p. 6 (bottom); © Time & Life Pictures/Getty Images, pp. 7, 9; © Eric Charbonneau/Getty Images, p. 8 (top); © NBC via Getty Images, p. 8 (bottom); © Djamilla Rosa Cochran/WireImage/Getty Images, p. 10; © Nancy Kaszerman/ZUMA Press, p. 11; © Ray Tamarra/Getty Images, p. 12 (top left); © Stephane Cardinale/People Avenue/CORBIS, p. 12 (top right); Neil Jordan/The Kobal Collection/Art Resource, NY, p. 12 (bottom); Warner Bros/Castle Rock/The Kobal Collection/Art Resource, NY, p. 13; © John Lamparski/Getty Images, p. 14; © iStockphoto.com/Kevin Winter, p. 15; © Johnny Nunez/WireImage/Getty Images, pp. 16, 28 (top left); © Rob Kim/Stringer/Getty Images, p. 17; AP Photo/StarPix/Amanda Schwab, p. 18; Tribeca Film/courtesy Everett Collection, p. 19 (top); © Ari Jankelowitz/Everett Collection, p. 19 (bottom); 20th Century Fox/Marvel/The Kobal Collection/Art Resource, NY, p. 20; © David Shankbone, pp. 21, 29 (top center); © Denis Makarenko/Dreamstime.com, p. 22 (top left); AP Photo/Matt Sayles, p. 22 (top right); © 20th Century Fox Film Corp. All rights reserved/courtesy Everett Collection, p. 23; © Alexandra Wyman/WireImage/Getty Images, p. 24; © Alberto E. Rodriguez/Getty Images, p. 25; © Alo Ceballos/FilmMagic/Getty Images, p. 26; © Gilbert Carrasquillo/Getty Images, p. 27; © Kevin Mazur/WireImage/Getty Images, p. 28 (right); © Lloyd Bishop/NBC via Getty Images, p. 28 (bottom left); © Sharkpixs/ZUMA Press, pp. 29 (top left), 29 (bottom); Joe Seer/Shutterstock.com, p. 29 (right).

Front cover: © Brian Killian/WireImage/Getty Images (left), © Stephen Lovekin/FilmMagic/Getty Images (right).
Back cover: © David Shankbone.

Main body text set in Shannon Std Book 12/18.
Typeface provided by Monotype Typography.